Lulu and Tuck Stories

WHAT'S A LEAP DAY?

Written & Illustrated By
Krishna Pandya

No More Blank Pages
© No More Blank Pages, LLC
www.nomoreblankpages.com

Copyright © 2023 by Krishna Pandya

All rights reserved. No part of this publication may be reproduced, distributed, transmitted, or used in any form without the prior written permission of the publisher, except for the use of brief quotations in a book review and certain other noncommercial uses permitted by copyright law.

For permission requests, email the publisher, at contact@nomoreblankpages.com

First paperback edition March 2023
ISBN: 978-1-957801-13-1

Illustrated by Krishna Pandya
Edited by Shruti Shukla

Published by No More Blank Pages, LLC
www.nomoreblankpages.com

This book belongs to:

_____

Create something you love!

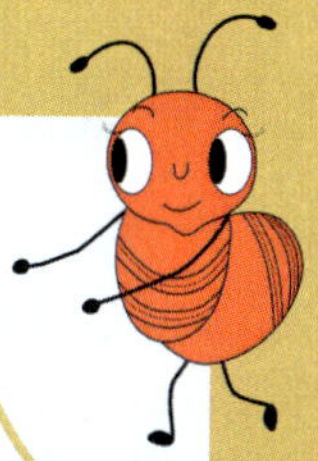

It is a bright February morning, still chilly.

The young animals of Forestland are at school!

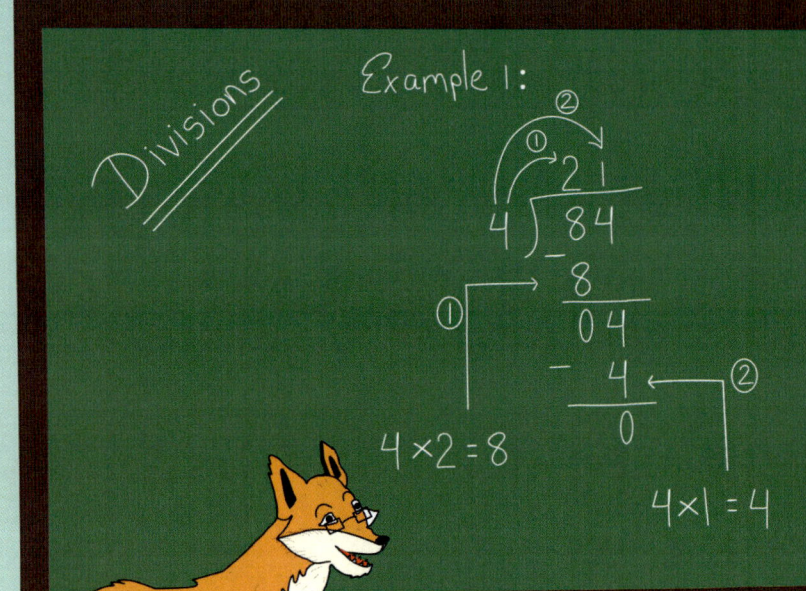

Mr. Zimba, the Fox, is teaching divisions today.

Lulu, the ant, is busy taking notes.

Her best friend Tuck, the elephant, seems puzzled looking at the board.

Mr. Zimba's class comes to a hold when the school principal Mrs. Pouch, a Kangaroo, walks in.

"Good morning, everyone!
I have someone I would like to introduce
to the class,"
Mrs. Pouch announces.

"Come in, dear," she calls out.

**A frog leaps his way in and says cheerfully,
"Hi! I am Leapling."**

"Leapling has just moved to Forestland,
and today is his first day at school."
Mrs. Pouch informs the class.

Mr. Zimba greets the newcomer and assigns him a desk next to Tuck.

"Hey, let me know if you need anything."
Tuck gives Leapling a warm welcome.

Usually, Tuck shares his book with Lulu
during the reading sessions.

But seeing Leapling confused,
Tuck teams with him instead.
Lulu seems unhappy about this.

During recess, Tuck steps out to use the restroom.
When he returns,
he finds his new friend
surrounded by other classmates.

"Leaaapliiingg?
What does that even mean?"
He overhears a mean voice.

They're asking Leapling
about his name, Tuck realizes.

"I was born on Leap Day,
that's why I was named Leapling."
He explains.

"Leap...what!?" Says one.

"Whatever... I don't think his name
has any meaning."
Says another.

Leapling is feeling lost.

Lulu knows that teasing is wrong,
but she fears that this new classmate
is trying to steal her best friend.

Feeling jealous,
Lulu joins others in making fun of Leapling.

"Don't trouble him, you guys."
Tuck tries to stop them.

When no one pays attention,
Tuck rushes to find Mr. Zimba.

Mr. Zimba yells as he enters the class,
"Quiet down at once... What's the matter?"

All the students move back to their seats in a jiffy.

Mr. Zimba calls a sad Leapling to stand next to him.

"This behavior is unacceptable,"
he expresses his disappointment to the class
in a firm voice.

"His name seems funny, huh?
Let me tell you the story!"
Mr. Zimba continues.

"Those born on a Leap Day,
on February 29, are called Leaplings or Leapers.
That's how he gets his name."

"But I thought there were only 28 days in February?"
Lulu asks confused.

"Leap year comes in every four years, Lulu.
It has 29 days in February instead of 28."
Mr. Zimba answers.

Regular Year
365 Days

Leap Year
366 Days

"This extra day is called
a Leap Day,
when our dear Leapling
was born,
on the 29th of February!"
Mr Zimba explains.

"So, Leapling's birthday comes
once in four years?"
Questions Tuck curiously.

Hearing Tuck's friendly voice,
Leapling responds,
"No, I celebrate on Feb 28 every year.
But yes, my real birthday comes once in four years."

"This year, I will get to celebrate it
on the actual day!" He adds.

The class finds the story of
Leapling's name super cool.
They feel embarrassed
for making fun of him.

Having realized her mistake,
Lulu apologizes quickly.
"Sorry Leapling! Sorry Mr. Zimba."

Others follow.

After learning how special
this birthday is for Leapling,
Tuck and Lulu decide
to plan a surprise party for him.

Lulu puts together a list
of all that needs to be done —

Decorations, food, games, music, and of course the Birthday cake...

Everyone in the class is given a task!

Tuck and Lulu are in charge of the games, and they have the perfect idea for their new friend.

It's the big day, February 29th!
The classroom is ready for the Birthday boy.

When Leapling enters,
all the animals shout at once, "SURPRISE!!"

There are so many decorations
and smiling faces,
Leapling's eyes cannot keep up.

Leapling looks at his friends in surprise.

He turns towards the board
and sees Happy Birthday in pretty, cursive words.

He jumps out of joy!
Everyone joins in the fun
and it turns into a dance party.

"IT'S GAME TIME!!"
Lulu's blasting voice grabs everyone's attention.

"The game is called..."
Lulu waits for Tuck to finish the sentence.

"Leap for the Cake!"
Tuck adds,
matching her enthusiasm.

Leap for the Cake

Lulu starts explaining the rules.

"Every time the music stops and
Tuck shouts a number,
Leapling has to leap
as far as he can to get to the cake."

"He will get ONLY FIVE CHANCES
to grab his sweet treat."

As Leapling gets excited for the game,
Lulu tells the main rule,
"You have to stay on the lily pads
while leaping, birthday boy.
If you touch the floor, you will have to start over."

At first, Leapling thinks that the game is easy...

But Tuck starts counting playfully, stopping whenever he wishes.

The floor rule makes the game even harder.

Round 4

After four chances, a bit of a struggle, and a lot of fun, Leapling finally makes it to the cake!

"That's how it's done!" Leapling shouts proudly.

Everyone sings the Happy-Birthday song as Leapling cuts his cake.

♪ Happy Birthday dear Leapling.....

As the students start to settle down
after the party,
Mr. Zimba reminds them,
"The next Leap Day
will come after four years, class...
don't forget."

"Yes guys, do remember my real Birthday!"
Leapling says joyfully
as he leaps around the class.

Everyone laughs with him this time,
and not at him.

"Leapling's name is the coolest!"
All cheer together!

About Krishna Pandya

Krishna lives in Northern Virginia with her husband. She was born in India and moved to the United States when she was 13. Krishna's love for the creative fields began in childhood with a mural of a beautiful bird her dad had created for her. She wrote her first poem in high school and has been creating it ever since. Receiving a bachelor's in Anthropology, 3 MBA's, and working in retail, corporate, non-profit, and government sectors have opened up her perspectives and creative thinking.

Today, she is the author, founder, and owner of No More Blank Pages and cites her nephew as one of the biggest inspirations to write children's poems and stories. She hopes to continue bringing forward beautiful, educational stories that kids can cherish for years!

Lulu and Tuck Stories

Lulu and Tuck Stories: What's Your New Year's Resolution?
Lulu and Tuck Stories: What's a Leap Day?
Lulu and Tuck Stories: Who is the Best Animal in Forestland?
Lulu and Tuck Stories: April Fool's Day Brings Lulu & Tuck Together
Lulu and Tuck Stories: Mother's Day with Mother Nature
Lulu and Tuck Stories: Teaching Lulu Not to Bully
Lulu and Tuck Stories: Lulu and Tuck Visit a Waterpark
Lulu and Tuck Stories: Lulu & Tuck Spread Smiles
Lulu and Tuck Stories: Lulu's Cleanup Mission
Lulu and Tuck Stories: Tuck Takes the Stage
Lulu and Tuck Stories: How Many Candies are Too Many Candies?
Lulu and Tuck Stories: Christmas on the Moon

Published Books

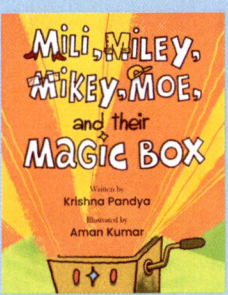

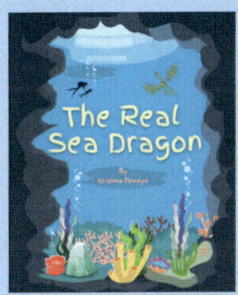

Mili, Miley, Mikey, Moe, and their Magic Box

Bee's First School Bus Ride

The Real Sea Dragon

Diwali at School with Raadhika

Monkey Stories

Lulu and Tuck Stories

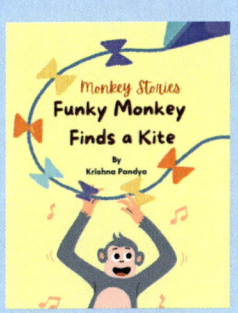
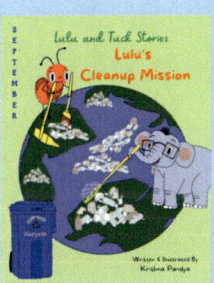
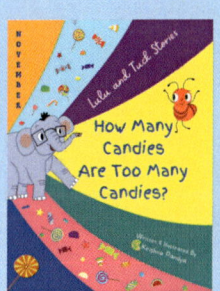
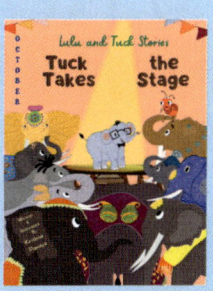

Greedy Monkey Learns a Lesson

Funky Monkey Finds a Kite

Lulu's Cleanup Mission

How Many Candies Are Too Many Candies

Tuck Takes the Stage

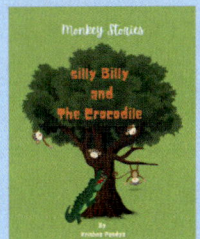

Silly Billy and The Crocodile

Available Now

Christmas on the Moon

What's Your New Year's Resolution?

Get your copy today!   www.nomoreblankpages.com   amazon

Made in United States
Orlando, FL
19 February 2024